CCSS **Genre** Realistic Fiction

Essential Question
What can traditions teach you about cultures?

The Special Meal

W9-BEZ-670

by Paul Mason
illustrated by Courtney Autumn Martin

CHAPTER 1
The Change of Plans

Estela jumped out of bed and dressed quickly. She was looking forward to her friend Vicky's pool party. They were going to swim and have a barbecue. All of her friends were going to be there.

Estela ran downstairs. Then she stopped. Her mom was putting the best tablecloth on the dining room table. It was the precious one from Puebla. They only used it to celebrate special events.

"You're up early," said her mother. "That's great. You can help me get ready for the family feast."

Estela's face dropped.

"But I was going over to Vicky's today," said Estela.

Mom shook her head. "I did remind you yesterday that Aunt Carmen, Uncle Felipe, and Grandpa and Grandma are coming over."

"Do I really have to be here?" asked Estela.

"I know this a disappointment," Mom said. "But family comes first. You'll have to let Vicky know."

"You can help Aunt Carmen in the kitchen," said Mom. "We are going to have a big meal. There's lots of cooking to do."

"I'd rather go to a pool party," Estela thought.

STOP AND CHECK

What is Estela's problem?

CHAPTER 2

Kitchen Duties

Aunt Carmen and Uncle Felipe arrived. They were carrying lots of bags.

Aunt Carmen gave Estela a big hug. "You've grown so much!" she said.

Estela looked at her feet.

"We've got lots to do in the kitchen," said Aunt Carmen. "I'm going to make mole poblano. I'm going to need your help."

Estela thought about the pool party. She sighed.

Estela helped Aunt Carmen take things out of the bags. She saw chilies, nuts, onions, garlic, lots of spices, and chocolate.

She also saw other things she didn't know.

There was so much. Estela wondered how they could all go into one sauce.

"How did you learn to make this sauce?" asked Estela.

"This is a family recipe," Aunt Carmen said with pride. "I learned it from my mother. She was a great cook. I loved to help her in the kitchen."

STOP AND CHECK

What is special about the dish they are making?

9

CHAPTER 3

Making Mole

Aunt Carmen put some spices into a bowl. It was Estela's job to crush them.

"That was my job when I was a girl," Aunt Carmen said. "Every Sunday, we had family dinners. It was a tradition to make this sauce." She looked at Estela. "And I always made a mess, too."

She laughed.
So did Estela.

Soon the thick, brown sauce was cooking. It smelled good. Aunt Carmen took out a spoonful. She gave it to Estela.

"Yum," said Estela. "This tastes delicious. Making mole is fun."

The doorbell rang. Grandpa and Grandma had arrived.

Grandpa put his head into the kitchen. "That smells good," he said.

"Did you help?" he asked Estela.

"She made most of it herself," Aunt Carmen said.

Estela smiled and blushed.

When they sat down to eat, the table was full of food. There were salads, beans, and plates of rice and turkey. Everyone was smiling and laughing. They were all happy to be with one another.

STOP AND CHECK

How is Estela feeling now?

13

CHAPTER 4

The Best Part

"Where's the mole poblano?" asked Grandpa.

Estela wanted to bring in the mole herself. But she didn't have the courage to carry the heavy dish.

"I'll get it," said Mom.

Estela watched them all spoon the sauce onto their plates.

"Yum!" said Grandpa, as everyone tasted it. The others all agreed.

Estela looked around the table. They were all so happy. Estela was glad she had stayed. This was better than a pool party. She enjoyed helping Aunt Carmen. And now she knew how to make a dish that her grandmother used to make. That felt great!

STOP AND CHECK

What did Estela learn that day?

Respond to Reading

Summarize

Use details from the story to summarize *The Special Meal*.

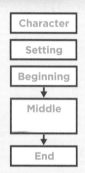

Text Evidence

1. How can you tell this story is realistic fiction? Genre

2. What happens to Estela at the beginning of the story? Sequence

3. Find *delicious* on page 11. What words and phrases help you figure out its meaning? Sentence Clues

4. Write about how Estela felt when her family ate the mole.

Write About Reading

Compare Texts
Read about mole sauce.

More about Mole

Chocolate on chicken? Wouldn't that taste strange?

Well, chocolate is just one of the things that go into mole. A mole sauce also includes chili peppers, nuts, onion, tomatoes, garlic, and spices. In fact, there can be 100 different ingredients in a mole.

Mole poblano is one of Mexico's most famous dishes and a symbol of Mexican culture. But there are many different recipes. Many families have their own recipes. Parents teach the recipe to their children.

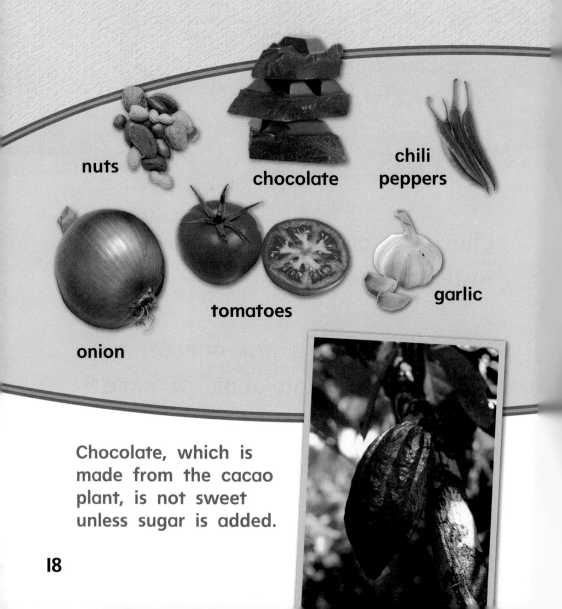

nuts

chocolate

chili peppers

onion

tomatoes

garlic

Chocolate, which is made from the cacao plant, is not sweet unless sugar is added.

It takes a long time to make mole sauce. Many of the ingredients are ground down to a fine powder before they are added to the recipe. The sauce cooks for many hours before it is ready to eat.

Mole is often eaten on special days. It is served at weddings, holidays, and big celebrations.

Burke Triolo Productions/Artville/Getty Images, D. Hurst/Alamy, Tetra Images/Getty Images, Author's Image/PunchStock.
...ing ...per...tock, stockbyte/Getty Images, Jupiterimages/FoodPix/Getty Images,

Make Connections

How did reading about the tradition of mole sauce help you understand Mexican culture? Essential Question

What Mexican traditions did you learn about from *The Special Meal* and *More About Mole?* Text to Text

Focus on Social Studies

Purpose To understand the place of traditions in a culture.

Procedure

 Step 1 Choose a special food that is traditional to a culture you know or can research.

Step 2 Make a poster that shows the special food and the things needed to make it.

Step 3 Write a short explanation of when and how the food is made. Explain why it is special for the culture.